How To Start A Successful Dog Walking Business In 10 Easy Steps

How To Start A Successful Dog Walking Business In 10 Easy Steps

A Walk the Walk Series Book

Volume 1

By Sarah-Jane White

This complete guide to how to set up a dog walking business takes you through all the aspects you need to consider to go from your lightbulb moment to taking your first pooch out for a stroll.

HOW TO START A SUCCESSFUL DOG WALKING BUSINESS IN 10 EASY STEPS

First edition. April 12, 2022.

ISBN: 978-1-7396503-1-5

Written by Sarah-Jane White.

Who is this book for?

This guide is for people who want to start a dog walking business with little or no previous experience.

DEDICATION

To my dog, who has been my loyal companion and biggest cheerleader throughout this process.
I couldn't have done it without you by my side.

Table of Contents

Are you eager to start your own business and work with dogs?

This is my Step-By-Step System For Starting Your Own Successful Dog Walking Business to go from earning £0 to £3,000 in 6 months.

In this book, I'm going to show you how to start a successful dog walking business from scratch. You don't need any prior experience and I'm going to break down everything you need to know step by step.

In this book you'll learn:

- How to quickly get up and running
- What rules and regulations you'll need to follow
- What paperwork you need (with free samples)
- How to market your business for FREE
- How much to charge to make a profit

Reliable dog walkers are always in demand. But to succeed in this competitive marketplace, you'll need more than just dog knowledge; you'll also need some business acumen.

If you're considering starting your own dog walking business, this book is for you. In it, I'll teach you everything you need to know to get started, from finding clients and setting rates to creating a marketing strategy and managing your finances. I'll also teach you how to walk dogs safely and effectively, so you can provide a top-notch service that will keep your clients coming back.

So whether you're a recent graduate looking for your first job, a stay-at-home parent looking for some extra income, or just someone who loves dogs and wants to turn their passion into a business, this book is for you.

In this book, you'll learn:

- How to start a dog walking business from scratch
- How to find clients and build relationships with them
- How to create a marketing strategy that will bring in new customers and keep them
- How to set rates and manage your finances
- How to walk dogs safely and effectively
- How to live the life you want

There are a number of benefits to running your own business, chief among them being the freedom and flexibility it offers. With your own business, you can set your own hours, choose the clients you work with, and make as much or as little money as you want. You're in control of your own destiny, and that's an incredibly empowering feeling.

Imagine what it would be like to do all this! Well, you could have the dog walking business of your dreams if you use the methods outlined in this book.

Of course, running your own business also comes with its own set of challenges. You'll need to be organised and self-motivated, and you'll need to wear a lot of different hats (marketer, salesperson, bookkeeper, etc.). But if you're up for the challenge, the rewards can be great.

Introduction

If you love dogs and are looking for a way to make some extra money, starting a dog walking business might be the perfect solution for you. Dog walking is a great way to get exercise and fresh air, while providing a valuable service to pet parents. Here are some tips on how to start a successful dog walking business.

1. Choose the right location: When choosing a location for your dog walking business, consider areas that have a high population of dogs. This will ensure that you have plenty of potential clients. You may also want to consider neighbourhoods that are close to parks or other outdoor areas where dogs can play safely.

2. Get licensed and insured: In order to legally operate your dog walking business, you will need to be licensed and insured. This may require a bit of paperwork, but it's well worth it in order to protect yourself and your clients.

3. Promote your services: Once you have your business up and running, it's important to promote your services in order to attract new clients. You can do this by posting flyers in local businesses, putting ads in the local newspaper or online, or even setting up a website or Facebook page for your business.

4. Offer a high-quality service: When starting a dog walking business, it's important to remember that you are competing with other businesses in your area. In order to be successful, you need to offer a high quality service that is worth the price. This means ensuring that your clients receive timely service, walking their dogs on a consistent basis, and providing regular updates on their dog's walks.

5. Stay organised: As with any business, it's important to stay organised in order to keep track of your finances and your dog walking schedule. Make sure you have a system for tracking client information, payments, and invoices. This will help ensure that your business runs smoothly.

I'll be exploring and explaining these in more detail in the following chapters including lots of tips on how to market your business for free!

Chapter One

Are you ready to set up a dog walking business?

Starting a business requires a lot of hard work and dedication, there will be many ups and downs and challenges but if you have the drive and enthusiasm, you're passionate about what you're doing and you plan ahead, it'll be worth it in the end.

Although you do not need a background in animal care, you must be confident around dogs and used to handling them when in public. You should have a high level of fitness, an organised mind, and good communications skills for dealing with dog owners.

So, before we get started, ask yourself these questions:

Do you have enough experience with dogs?

While you may love spending time with your own dog, that doesn't necessarily mean you have the experience needed to professionally walk other people's dogs. Dog walking is more than just taking a leisurely stroll around the block. Professional dog walkers need to be able to handle all types of breeds, personalities, and behaviour problems.

They also need to be aware of local leash laws and be able to keep both the dog and the owner happy. If you're not sure you have the experience needed to be a professional dog walker, consider volunteering at your local animal shelter or taking a dog training class. Once you have some experience under your belt, you'll be able to decide if professional dog walking is the right career for you.

Do you have the time to devote to a business?

Starting a new business is an exciting and challenging undertaking. However, it is also important to be realistic about the time commitment that is required. Before embarking on this journey, ask yourself if you have the time to devote to the planning and execution of your business plan. Keep in mind that a successful business takes a lot of hard work and dedication.

If you are not prepared to put in the long hours, then you may want to reconsider starting a new business. However, if you are willing to make the commitment, then there is no limit to what you can achieve. With careful planning and a lot of hard work, you can turn your dreams into reality.

Do you have the financial resources to start and maintain a business?

Before starting a business, it is important to assess your financial situation and make sure you have the resources in place to sustain a long-term venture. This includes not only start-up costs, but also ongoing expenses such as inventory, marketing, and employee salaries. If you do not have the cash on hand to cover these costs, you will need to secure funding through loans or investment.

Additionally, you should have a clear understanding of your personal financial goals and how owning a business will impact your ability to achieve them. For example, are you looking to generate income to support yourself and your family? Or are you hoping to build long-term wealth through franchising? By taking the time to understand your financial needs and goals, you can make sure that starting a business is the right decision for you.

What are your long-term career goals?

When starting a new business, it is important to have a clear idea of your long-term goals. What do you hope to achieve in the next five years? In the next ten years? By setting realistic goals and milestones, you can measure your progress and ensure that your business is on track to meet your desired objectives.

Additionally, having long-term goals will help you make important decisions about the direction of your business. For example, if you are hoping to grow your business quickly, you may need to invest in marketing and expansion. However, if you are content with a slower pace of growth, you can focus on profitability and cash flow. By understanding your long-term goals, you can make sure that your business is headed in the right direction.

Are you prepared to deal with the challenges of owning a business?

Owning a business is not always easy. There will be ups and downs, and you will need to be prepared for the challenges that come with running a company. This includes everything from managing cash flow to dealing with client complaints. If you are not prepared to handle these challenges, you may want to reconsider starting a business.

Dealing with the challenges of owning a business can be difficult, but it is also one of the most rewarding experiences you will ever have. If you are prepared to put in the hard work, you can achieve your dreams and build a successful company.

⇨ TASK: Write down your answers and how you feel about each of the questions above

Seven characteristics of successful dog walking business owners

There are some essential qualities that all successful dog walking business owners share. Here are seven of them:

1. **Passion for Dogs** – This is probably the most important characteristic because it will keep you motivated when things get tough. You need to love dogs and enjoy being around them, even when they're being naughty!

2. **Patience** – Handling dogs can be unpredictable, so you need to have plenty of patience when dealing with them.

3. **Good Physical Condition** – A lot of the work involved in dog walking is quite obviously physical, so you need to be in good shape.

4. **Enthusiasm** – A positive attitude is key when it comes to dealing with clients and their pets. No one wants to work with a grumpy person!

5. **Strong Communication Skills** – Good communication is essential when working with both clients and other dog walkers.

6. **Confidence and Determination** – It takes a lot of guts to start your own business, but you also need to be determined to make it work.

7. **Knowledge of Dog Behaviour** – It's helpful to have some understanding of dog behaviour in order to provide the best possible service.

Dog walking can be a competitive industry, so you'll need to have a good head for business if you want to be successful.

⇨ CHECKPOINT: Do you have these qualities? If not, are you prepared to do what it takes to get them?

Chapter Two

Market Research

Do your market research and decide who is your ideal client

It’s important to do some market research before starting your business and to figure out who your ideal client is. This will help you focus your marketing efforts and attract the right type of client.

Competitive Research

In order to get ahead of the competition, it’s important to know what they’re doing. This means spending some time researching your local dog walking businesses and seeing what you're up against.

Create a spreadsheet and record the following info:

1. **What is their business called?**- This is important because you want a unique name for your business and you don't want to use a name already out there and suffer potential legal action for infringing on someone's name or trademark.

2. **What services do they offer?** - List the services you find on their website or Facebook page. This will give you an overview of what they offer and may give you ideas for how to package your services. It might even give you inspiration for additional services that could bring extra revenue to your business.

3. **How much do they charge?** - Write down their costs for single walks, group walks and prices for any extras like training or house sitting. This will help you to price your services competitively.

4. **What areas do they cover?** - This will give you an idea of how saturated an area is with dog walkers and will help you spot potential gaps so you know where to focus your marketing efforts and pick up clients. This can be plotted on a Google map to help you visualise their coverage.

5. **What days/times do they operate?** - This will help you understand their working hours so you'll know what hours you may need to cover. It will also help you spot any gaps that you may be prepared to fill in.

6. **How they market themselves** - Try googling their name and seeing what shows up in the search results. This will give you a clue as to where they may have listed their business or are running adverts. Check out their social media pages and website too as often this is where people will be promoting their offers.

By doing this research, you'll be able to see what the competitive landscape looks like and how you can make your own business stand out from the crowd. It will also give you insight into how you can start marketing your business as soon as you are ready in a strategic and effective way with a limited budget.

⇨ TASK: Do your competitor research

What is your unique selling point?

As a dog walker, it's important to stand out from the competition. After all, there are plenty of people who are willing to take your potential clients' furry friends for a walk.

So, how can you make sure that you're the one they choose? It all comes down to finding your unique selling point.

By this, we mean what makes you different? Why should someone pay you to walk their dog, instead of the next dog walking business? Consider how you can differentiate your dog walking services from your competition.

Think about what sets you apart from other dog walkers in your area. Think about what value you add for your clients.

For example:

- Do you have experience with large breeds? Small breeds? Puppies? Older dogs?

- Do you have extensive experience working with dogs with specific temperaments, like anxiety?

- Are you certified in canine first aid?

- Do you offer special services like training or behaviour modification?

- Perhaps you can offer different hours, different routes or group walks that your competition does not offer.

- Consider your walking route. Do you have a regular route that you take all of your clients on? Or do you tailor your walks to each individual dog's needs?

- Do you provide pick-up and drop-off services? Dog sitting services? Daily updates on how their dog did on the walk?

Once you've pinpointed what makes you unique, be sure to highlight it in your marketing materials. Let potential clients know why they should choose you over the competition.

If you can find a way to differentiate yourself from the competition, you'll be in a much better position to win clients away from them.

Whatever your strategy, make sure you know what makes your business unique and then you can focus on communicating that to potential clients.

⇨TASK: Write down three sentences about what makes your business different and why people should choose you.

Chapter Three

Finding Your Ideal client

Now you've done some research and worked out what you might offer, it's time to think about who you want as a client and whether they match.

Ideal Client Profile

An Ideal Client Profile (ICP) is a detailed description of your perfect client. Developing an ICP can help you better understand your target market and make more strategic decisions about your marketing and sales efforts. Let's keep it simple so, when thinking about who your ideal client is, you should consider the following factors:

Lifestyle: What is their lifestyle like? Do they work long hours or travel a lot? If so, they may need someone to walk their dog for them.

Location: Are they local to you? This will make it easier for you to meet them and for them to get to know you.

Needs: Do they have young children who are too busy to walk their dog? Or are they retired and would like someone to take their dog for a walk each day? Do they have training needs for their dog? What support do they need at their time of life with their dog? How can you help them?

Budget: How much do they need to pay for your services? Remember, you need to make a profit!

By focusing on your ideal client, you can target your marketing specifically to those people, saving you time and money. Join special interest online groups where dog owners hang out so you can see the sorts of questions dog owners might ask you and you can learn about your local dog owners and what they need help with.

➪ TASK: Write down your ideal client profile using the criteria above.

Chapter Four

Your business name and logo

When starting a new business, one of the first steps is to come up with a name. There are a few things to consider when generating a business name for a dog walking business. The name you choose should be reflective of the products or services you offer, and it should be memorable and easy to pronounce.

Avoid using complex words or phrases that will be difficult for potential clients to recall. The name should be unique enough to stand out from the competition. With so many dog walking businesses on the market, it's important to choose a name that will make you stand out from the pack.

For your dog walking business, you'll want to choose a name that highlights your love of dogs and your dedication to providing quality care. Here are a few tips to help you generate the perfect name for your business:

1. Start by brainstorming a list of words that describe your business. These could be words like "loyal," "trusted," "pawsome," or "woof-tastic."

2. Once you have a list of descriptive words, try adding them together to create compound words or phrases. For example, "Pawsome Dog Walking" or "Woof-tastic Dog Walks."

3. Consider the geographic area you'll be serving. A name like "Richmond Park Paws" would work well for a dog walking business based in Central London, while "Tail Waggin' Adventures" might be more fitting for a company based in a rural area.

4. If you're having trouble coming up with a name on your own, consider using a word generator tool online to help.

Your business name is one of the most important branding tools you have. It needs to be catchy, memorable and representative of what you do. Spend some time brainstorming a list of possible names and ask your friends and family for their opinions.

Be warned though, if you ask for an opinion, you'll get one. Often people interpret the question 'What do you think of this?' as 'What's wrong with this?' and you will find negative comments and harsh criticisms rather than constructive responses!

Instead, ask them 'How can I improve on this name?' and you'll get much better advice, or none at all which can be just as helpful!

Consider how your name will appeal to your ideal client too. For example, if you are targeting older dog owners, you might want to avoid anything too quirky that would be difficult for them to remember.

When you've got a shortlist of names you like don't forget to do the following:

1. Make sure the domain name is available. You can do this by going to a domain name registrar like 123 Reg and typing the name into the search bar. If it's available, you can register it there and then.

2. Check if the name is already trademarked. You can do this by searching on the government's Intellectual Property Office website. If it's not trademarked, you are in a better position. But just because a name isn't trademarked doesn't mean it's not being used.

3. Register your business with Companies House if you are setting up a limited business. This is an easy process to do online and will give you an official company registration number which you can use on your marketing materials. But most people starting out will be sole-traders so you need to tell HRMC that you are self-employed.

4. Create a logo. A professional-looking logo will help to legitimise your business and make it look more credible to potential clients. You can get a logo designed for a few pounds by a professional graphic designer on places like Fiverr, or you can use a free online logo maker, like Canva. Be careful if

using a free design tool as you will not own the copyright to the logo and it is highly likely that another business will be using it too!

⇨ TASK - Have fun and generate a list of names for your business

Registering your business

Tell the taxman. All businesses must register their business with HMRC within 3 months of trading – that means within 90 days of taking your first payment. You can set up as a sole trader or a limited company and each has its own pros and cons, so get an accountant's advice to help you make the right decision from the outset. You can get more information on UK Government's website for the different options and the processes for each.

⇨ TASK - Tell the taxman

Chapter Five

Insurance

Insurance requirements for a dog walking business

If you're thinking of starting a dog walking business, you'll need to make sure you're properly insured. Insurance is mandatory for protecting both your business and your client's interests. The type of insurance you'll need will vary depending on the size and scope of your operation, but there are some general requirements you'll need to meet.

First, you'll need liability insurance to protect yourself in case a client's dog is injured while in your care. This is essential in covering any medical bills or other damages that may be incurred. This is especially important if you're planning on walking multiple dogs at once, as the risk of an accident is increased.

You'll also need to make sure you have public liability insurance, as this will cover you if a member of the public is injured by a dog under your care, or the dog causes an accident. This is particularly important if you're planning on walking dogs in busy areas or parks.

If you use your car or home as part of your dog walking business, you must inform your insurance companies – an additional premium may be payable. It's important to note that standard home insurance policies will not cover businesses, so you may need to take out a separate policy.

If your dog walking business grows and you need people to work for you, then you should also opt for Employer's Liability Insurance.

Summary of Insurance Cover Needed for a Dog Walking Business

Public Liability

Usually, you can choose between £1 million to £10 million worth of cover to protect your business against claims arising from injury to a member of the public or for damage to their property.

Key Cover

You are protected against incurring the cost of new keys, replacement locks, resetting intruder alarms and calling out charges in the event that you lose a client's keys. If you hold the keys to your client's properties, you will also need a Criminal Record Bureau (CRB) check.

Care, Custody & Control

This will cover the animals in your care in case you lose them or they sustain an injury whilst in your care. It also covers illness or death of that animal in your care, custody or control or that of any of your staff.

Equipment Cover

Cover for your equipment against theft, loss and accidental damage.

Employers' Liability

If you employ anyone to help with your dog walking business, you must have this insurance by law. The minimum level of cover you must have is £5 million, but some insurers will offer up to £10 million.

Close Family Cover

Some insurance providers offer to include your close family members under your standard policy. This means that if you employ your husband, wife, son, daughter or any other close family, you do not need to take out Employers' Liability.

Personal Accident Cover equipment

This covers you for loss of earnings and any medical expenses as a result of an accident. It will also pay out a lump sum if you are permanently disabled or killed as a result of an accident.

Business Interruption Cover

This covers you for any loss of earnings as a result of your business being disrupted, for example, by damage to your vehicle or your illness.

Product Liability

This covers you for any claims arising from products or services you have supplied which have caused injury or damage. This could include dog food, toys or leads.

How Much Does Dog Walking Insurance Cost?

The cost of your insurance will depend on a number of factors, including the type of policy you choose, the level of cover you need and the area you live in. You may be able to get a discount if you buy a policy that covers multiple types of insurance, such as public liability and employer's liability. It's important to shop around and compare policies to make sure you're getting the best deal. You can do this by using an insurance broker or searching online. When you're looking for quotes, make sure you provide accurate information about your business, as this will affect the price you're quoted. For example, if you say you only walk one dog at a time but you actually sometimes walk two or more, this could invalidate your policy.

➪ TASK - Take out insurance and CRB check

Chapter Six

Rules and Regulations

Regulations for a dog walking business

As with all businesses there are rules and regulations. But unlike many professions, dog walking does not have any requirements for dog walkers to have a dog walking licence, qualification, or certification. With no minimum requirements to regulate them, all you need to start a successful dog walking company is a passion for dogs and enough free time and this book!

However, there are laws that cover dogs and behaviour so you need to know what they are and how they affect you.

It's worth noting that there are no legal limits on the number of dogs you can walk at once but be aware that it is generally advised to walk no more than four at a time and each must be on its own lead. You need to be fully in control of all the dogs and a pack of dogs together can become very excitable. Check with your local council and any parks that you plan to walk in what specific rules you need to comply with.

These are the main acts that govern dog walking in the UK and what they mean for you as a dog walker:

Animal Welfare Act 2006

The Act protects all domestic animals including dogs. The law states that a dog's owner is always held responsible for them. A dog walker is also regarded as being responsible for the dog - while he or she is in command of it. As a result, a dog walker may be held criminally liable under the Act.

The Control of Dogs Order 1992

Dogs in public must wear a collar that has the owner's name and address on it.

The Road Traffic Act 1988

On highways, dogs must be on a leash at all times. If your dog is hurt in a vehicle accident, the driver is responsible for stopping and giving you their information.

The Dangerous Dogs Act 1991 and Amendment 1997

You must be in control of the dog at all times as it is against the law for a dog to be 'dangerously out of control' in a public place.

If the dog does not come when called, if it chases, barks at or jumps up at other people, you could receive complaints. Gov.uk has more information on controlling your dog in public.

Dogs (Protection of Livestock) Act 1953

If you are walking the dog across farmland, be aware that your dog must not worry the livestock. A farmer is within their rights to shoot any dog that causes problems to their livestock, so be incredibly careful in farmland areas.

Dog Fouling - The Clean Neighbourhoods and Environment Act 2005

You must clean up any dog faeces or you could face a fine of up to £1000. Make sure you have plenty of biodegradable poop bags and dispose of them properly.

Transporting dogs in your vehicle

When you are dog walking, there will be times when you need to transport the dog in your car. The law requires that all dogs must be suitably restrained while in a moving vehicle. This means your vehicle will need to be fitted with suitable dog crates to ensure that the welfare of the dog is safeguarded and that they are not at any risk of injury.

Dogs must have adequate ventilation and temperature control with water available in their crate too. Dogs must not be left unattended in your vehicle other than whilst you are collecting or dropping off. The vehicle must be locked if you leave it unattended.

From a hygiene point of view, your vehicle must be capable of being cleaned and disinfected regularly, this is especially important if you have had a dog on board with a disease, or parasites such as fleas.

In summary

So, to sum up, in order to comply with the law as a dog walking business in the UK, you need to make sure that your dogs are always on a lead and under control, that you pick up their faeces, and that you don't let them worry livestock. If you follow these regulations, you should be good to go!

⇨ CHECKPOINT - Are you familiar with the rules and regulations?

Chapter Seven

Money - Costs and Charges

Set up costs for your dog walking business

How much should you budget to get started? Well, you will need at minimum the right insurance, some equipment such as leads, harnesses, toys and you'll need to do some marketing.

1. Insurances - £100
2. CRB Check - £30
3. Equipment and supplies. - £100
4. Marketing - £250

This is the bare minimum to get you going, once you're underway you can then invest in branded clothing, vehicle signwriting and joining an organisation like the National Association of Pet Sitters and Dog Walkers (NarpsUK).

Equipment & transport

You need to be able to collect dogs and take them to where you plan to walk them. If you are walking a few dogs at the same time, you might need a van for your dog walking business. Alternatively, you can use your own car and claim mileage and cleaning costs against your tax.

You will also need leads, harnesses and some toys such as a ball thrower and tug toys to keep your charges amused whilst you are out and about. Consumables include dog treats and eco-friendly poop bags.

A pet first aid kit is also a good idea as accidents do happen. Include items such as bandages, hydrogen peroxide (to clean wounds), cotton wool, a tick remover tool and latex gloves.

You can purchase all of this equipment from your local pet store or alternatively, many companies online stock everything you need and will deliver it to your door.

Clothing

You're going to be outside in all conditions and having the right clothing will make all the difference to your comfort. Even on the sunniest days, it's worth taking a waterproof jacket as you know how unpredictable the British weather can be!

Weather-appropriate trousers are essential too. Jeans are hard wearing but not always comfortable. Brands like Craighoppers make wind and waterproof gear that's ideal for dog walking.

Invest in a good pair of walking boots too as you'll be doing a lot of walking! And in winter, you'll want some waterproof country boots (not wellies they'll give you blisters).

Clothing Checklist

- Sturdy walking boots
- Warm down long coat
- Hat and scarf
- Gloves
- Waterproof boots with thick socks (country boots) for wet wintry days
- Waterproof jacket
- T-Shirt or branded polo shirts - free advertising!
- Sweatshirt/ branded hoodie with pockets (always helpful)
- Long sleeve t-shirts for Spring/Autumn
- Jeans - practical and hardwearing - wear thermals underneath them for winter
- Sun hat or baseball cap

Initial Marketing

When you're starting out you'll need to do plenty of marketing, but this doesn't need to cost the earth. Armed with some initial business cards and flyers you can get going very quickly thanks to the power of the internet and your local community.

One of the best ways to market your business is to create a free website on Wordpress.com and list your services. You can also post flyers in local businesses and dog parks. You can also offer your first few clients a discount to encourage them to spread the word about your business. In addition, be sure to take advantage of social media by creating profiles on sites like Facebook and Twitter. By following these simple tips, you can get your dog walking business off to a great start without breaking the bank.

I've written a whole chapter full of ways to market your business for free (see Chapter Eleven).

Setting your prices: How much do I charge?

You've checked out what your local competition is charging – (many dog walkers will put this information on their websites, so it's not hard to get hold of if you haven't found it yet). It's a good idea to set your dog walking prices in the middle of where your competition is – too low and people will think your service is poor, too high and you may price many potential clients out. If the hourly rates for dog walking services are between £10-20, set yours at £17.

⇨ TASK - Set your startup budget and work out your prices

Chapter Eight

Your Paperwork

Paperwork, the records and information you'll need to keep

In order to run a successful dog walking business, you need to be well organised and have a system for tracking your finances and scheduling dog walks. This will help ensure that your business runs smoothly. Record keeping is a vital part of running a business. Without accurate and up-to-date records, it would be difficult to track income and expenses, monitor dogs and clients, or measure performance against objectives.

There are many different types of business records that need to be kept, and some of the most important include financial statements, invoices, receipts, and contracts. Financial statements provide an overview of a business's financial health, while invoices and receipts can be used to track income and expenses. Contracts are important for documenting agreements with suppliers, clients, and employees. By establishing a system for keeping accurate records, businesses can operate more efficiently and effectively.

Keeping records for your business is important to protect you and your clients. You'll need a new client intake form, a services contract, and a key release form at minimum. I have a free dog walking contract to get you started on my resources page on my website (link in the Resources at the end of this book). You might also need a dog training agreement if you offer training on walks too.

Dog walking and client records

You need to keep records of your clients, including contact information, addresses, and the services you provide. Plus details on their dogs that they provided you.

Make sure you have accurate records of each dog's name, age, breed, and any special instructions from the owner. This will help you to provide the best possible service to your clients.

You should keep records of which dogs you walked and when so that you can accurately invoice your clients.

If anything unusual happens whilst you are walking a dog, make a written note of it as soon as the event as possible so that you can later recall accurately if needed.

You should track the following information about your clients at the very least:

1. **Client Information** – Name, Address, Phone Number, Email Address, Dog Details.
2. **Invoice Information** – Date of Invoice, Client Name, Service Provided, Amount Charged.
3. **Payment Information** – Date of Payment, Amount Paid, Method of Payment (Cash, Check, Credit Card).
4. **Walk Log** – Date, Time, Duration of Walk, Type of Walk (Regular or One-Time), Address of Walk.

Dog walk schedule

You should also create a schedule for your dog walks. This will help you plan your day and ensure that all your clients are serviced. The following information should be included in your walk schedule:

1. Client name
2. Dog name
3. Type of Walk (Regular, One-Off, Group)
4. Address of pickup and drop off
5. Route
6. Start Time
7. End Time
8. Duration of Walk

You can use your mobile phone to track walks, and some dogs may have a GPS tracker which will tell their owner where they have been too. I have included some recommended apps and trackers on the Resources page on my website to help.

⇨ TASK: Decide how to keep client information and set up your system

Finances & Bookkeeping

When starting a new business, it's important to understand the basics of bookkeeping and accounting. This will help you track income and expenses, prepare financial statements, and file taxes. There are many resources available to help you get started, including books and online courses.

You should also open a business bank account to keep your personal and business finances separate. This will make it easier to track expenses and prepare financial statements. And, if you ever need to apply for a loan or line of credit, having a business bank account will give you a better chance of being approved.

To keep track of your income and expenses, you can use a simple spreadsheet or sign up for accounting software like QuickBooks or FreshBooks. These tools will help you track your finances, generate invoices, and manage your clients.

When it comes to taxes, you will need to file a business tax return each year. This is in addition to your personal tax return. To make sure you are complying with the law, you should speak to an accountant or tax specialist.

Equipment and expenses

If you have any equipment, tools or vehicles for your business, keep a log of all maintenance and repairs along with associated costs. This will come in handy at tax time as you can deduct these expenses.

You should also track any business expenses you have as you can claim these back on your taxes as well. This includes equipment, uniform, treats and mileage if you use your own vehicle to travel to clients' homes or dog walking spots. Keep the receipts from any purchases of equipment so you can offset them on your tax return.

Marketing expenses

You should also keep track of how much money you are spending on advertising and marketing so that you can gauge the return on investment (ROI).

Business licences and permits

Keep your licences and permits to hand. Depending on your location and the services you offer, you may need to obtain certain business licences and permits. For example, if you will be walking dogs in a public park, you may need a permit from the local authorities. If you plan to board dogs in your home, you may need to obtain a kennel licence. Check with your local council office to find out what licences and permits are required in your area.

Invoicing your clients

When it comes to billing, some dog walkers prefer to be paid weekly or bi-weekly, while others choose to be paid after each walk. There is no right or wrong answer here, it really depends on what works best for you and your clients.

Some dog walkers also offer package deals whereby the client pays a certain amount upfront for a set number of walks per week/month. This can be a great way to guarantee a certain income each month.

Keep copies of all invoices you send because you will need these for your taxes.

Ensure all data is held securely in accordance with GDPR legislation

As more and more businesses move online, it is essential that they take steps to ensure that all data is held securely in accordance with GDPR legislation. There are a number of things that businesses can do to protect data, such as encrypting sensitive information and ensuring that only authorised personnel have access to it. They should also have procedures in place for dealing with data breaches, such as notifying affected individuals and taking steps to prevent further breaches. By taking these measures, businesses can protect both themselves and their clients from the risks associated with data insecurity.

⇨ TASK: Set up your system for recording your financial information and bookkeeping

Chapter Nine

Your first client

Client on-boarding

When a client contacts you looking for dog walking services, you should send them your new client intake form which enables you to gather details of the owner (s) and the dog. Before signing a contract with the client, you should meet them with their dog to make sure you are a good fit for each other.

What questions to ask a dog owner who is looking for a dog walker-

- How many dogs do you have that need walking?

- Where are their favourite dog walking spots within your area of operation?

- When do you need me to walk the dog on a daily basis (morning/afternoon)?

- Which days of the week would be best for arranging walks (2/3 days)?

- What is your preferred contact method? Email/text message/phone call?

- What other services do you require such as feeding or providing medication to your pet?

Client communications

How will you communicate with your clients? If you can be flexible to your clients needs, that is ideal – different people prefer to communicate in different ways – phone call, email, text or WhatsApp are likely to be most common. If this is tricky for you and you can only communicate in a specific way, include that in your contract of services so your client is clear from the outset how communications will be managed.

Dealing with issues

What happens if something goes wrong? Hopefully nothing, but you should always be prepared. What if a dog escapes from your care? What if you're injured and can't walk a dog? These are unlikely scenarios, but it's best to plan for them anyway. Include a clause in your contract so that you are covered, and make sure you have public liability insurance in case of any accidents.

If something does happen, be honest with the owner – if they later find out that you weren't truthful, the trust will be broken.

If you believe that the problem was your fault, then offer to remediate – you may need to claim on your insurance.

If the problem was not your fault, try to get witnesses to corroborate your story. You might like to wear a body cam to record the walks - something like a small GoPro is ideal and can be fixed to a hat or your chest.

⇨ TASK: Get your client intake form and contract paperwork prepared.

Chapter Ten

Walking someone else's dog

How to walk dogs safely

As a new professional dog walker, you will likely be called upon to walk a new dog for the first time at some point. While this may be daunting, there are some simple steps you can follow to make sure the experience goes smoothly for both you and the dog.

First, it is important to introduce yourself to the dog in a calm and friendly manner. Allow the dog to sniff you and get comfortable with your presence before attempting to put on a leash. Once the leash is attached, take things slowly at first, letting the dog get used to walking with you. If the dog seems hesitant or fearful, try using positive reinforcement in the form of treats or praise.

Make sure you have a good grasp on the leash. You don't want the dog to be able to pull away from you, but you also don't want to hold the leash too tightly, as this could hurt the dog. Don't wrap it around your hand as if the dog does pull you could be injured. Watch out for long lines too as they can get tangled around your ankles and cause severe burns.

Second, be aware of your surroundings at all times. Watch for potential hazards, such as cars or other animals, and keep the dog away from them.

Always be prepared to pick up after the dog. This means having poop bags handy to store the waste in.

Finally, be sure to pay attention to the dog's body language and cues; if the dog seems uncomfortable or wants to go home, it is probably time to end the walk.

The first time you walk a new dog, you might want to keep the walk short so that the dog doesn't have too much time with an unfamiliar person. If possible, have the owner come with you on the first walk so that they can show you how the dog likes to be walked.

Walking multiple dogs from different households

Walking multiple dogs from different households can be a challenging but rewarding experience. It is important to remember that each dog has its own individual temperament, energy level, and set of obedience commands that they are used to following. As such, it is important to take the time to get to know each dog before attempting to walk them together.

Once you have a good understanding of each dog's personality and behaviours, you can begin working on walking them in a group. Start by walking the dogs in pairs, making sure that they are comfortable with each other's presence. Once they are used to being around each other, you can introduce another dog.

Although there are no laws about how many dogs to walk at once, 4 is suggested as the maximum for safety. For you and the dogs.

Chapter Eleven

Marketing Ideas

Marketing your new dog walking business

So you are all set now and ready for a client, but how do people find out about you?

As a new dog walker, then you know that marketing your business can be tough. It can be hard to get people to trust you when they don't even know who you are. In this chapter, I will give you some tips on how to market your dog walking business for free! I'll show you how to get your name out there and bring in more clients without spending a penny. Just put in the time and effort, and you'll see results!

The internet is a powerful tool that can help you market your business for free. If you don't have a website, now is the time to create one. You can use your website to write about your services and post photos of your happy clients. Be sure to include your contact information so potential clients can reach you.

Social media is also a great way to get the word out about your dog walking business. Set up your page and then head to your local groups where you can interact with dog owners.

Don't forget about old-fashioned methods of marketing, too. Writing an article for your local newspaper is a great way to get exposure for your business. You can talk about the benefits of dog walking and why it's important to choose a reputable dog walker.

With a little time and effort, you can market your dog walking business for free and reach a wide audience of potential clients. Just be creative and think outside the box!

Let's get down to some specifics...

Google My Business

Google My Business is a free and easy-to-use tool for businesses and organisations to manage their online presence across Google, including Search and Maps. By verifying and editing your business information, you can help clients find you, contact you, and learn more about your business.

To get started using Google My Business for your dog walking business, create or claim your business listing. Once your listing is verified, you can start managing your business information, including your hours of operation, location, contact information, and more. You can also post updates and photos to show clients and prospects what's new with your business. In addition, you can use your listing to respond to reviews and messages from clients.

To get the most out of Google My Business, it's important to keep your information up to date and complete. clients are more likely to contact businesses with complete listings, and you can use your listing to show off your dog walking business's best features. Be sure to include:

- A description of your business and services

- Your business hours
- A link to your website
- Your business location
- Contact information
- Photos and videos

By taking the time to fill out your Google My Business listing, you can help clients find your dog walking business and learn more about what you have to offer. In addition, you can use your listing to connect with clients and build relationships.

A verified listing will also help with people finding you as your business will be displayed higher up in the search results. You can get your business verified by postcard or phone. The steps to verify your business are different depending on whether you have a new or existing listing.

To get verified, sign in to Google My Business and select the listing you'd like to verify. Click Verify now and follow the prompts.

Create a Free Website with Google Sites

Websites aren't absolutely necessary, but they do lend an air of credibility to your business. 80% of consumers search online before making a purchase or using a new service, so if you can't be found online, this could put potential clients off.

In order to promote your business, you need to create a professional-looking website. This will give clients a chance to learn more about you, see photos of your work and read testimonials from happy clients.

Be sure to include your contact information on your website and link your social media profiles. This is your shop window, so it's important to make sure it looks good. Make sure the layout is easy to navigate, the text is easy to read and the images are high quality.

Creating a website used to be a complex and time-consuming task that required a degree of technical expertise.

However, thanks to the advent of user-friendly website builders, it is now possible for anyone to create a professional-looking website without any need for coding or other technical skills.

One of the most popular website builders is Google Sites, which offers a free and easy-to-use platform for creating websites.

To get started with Google Sites, simply create a free account and then follow the prompts to choose a template and start adding content. You can add text, images, videos, and other elements to your website with just a few clicks. There's even a template for a dog walker to get you started!

And if you ever need help, there is a wealth of online resources available to guide you through the process.

Start a blog

A blog can be a great way to promote your dog walking business. By sharing your love of dogs and your experience as a dog walker, you can attract new clients and build trust with potential clients. In addition, a blog can help you to stand out from the competition by showcasing your unique approach to dog walking.

Whether you focus on tips for choosing the right dog walker or stories about the adventures you and your furry clients have had, a well-written blog can give potential clients a taste of what it would be like to work with you. If you're looking for article ideas, a good source is from the questions you're being asked by your clients.

So if you're looking for a new way to bring in business, consider starting a blog about your dog walking adventures. You can use a platform like blogger.com for free.

Use your local library

There are a number of ways to advertise at a low cost (or sometimes free) in your local library.

One is to take advantage of the notice board. Most libraries have at least one bulletin board where community members can post flyers and other information. You can also talk to the library staff about adding your flyer to the bulletin board or placing it in a designated area for community announcements. There may be a nominal charge of £5 a month, but it's worth it.

Another way to advertise for free in your local library is to host an event. Many libraries have meeting rooms or other spaces that can be rented for a small fee. You can use this space to host a book reading, lecture, or another event that will promote your business. Maybe you could run one about how to fit a harness properly to your dog? Or review some dog products that people might find interesting. Why not team up with someone who can teach Canine First Aid basics?

Finally, you can also take advantage of the library's resources to create your own marketing materials. Many libraries offer free access to computers, printers, and other equipment that can be used to create flyers, business cards, and other marketing materials.

Facebook

There are a number of ways to advertise for free using Facebook. One option is to create a business page. This will allow you to share information about your product or service with a wide audience.

Another way to reach potential clients is by joining relevant Facebook groups. This will give you access to people with similar interests, who may be interested in what you have to offer. You can join some groups as your page and be sure to check out their rules too as you don't want to get booted out for advertising. Instead, try to be helpful and post interesting content related to dogs, dog walking and care.

You can use Facebook events to promote your business. By creating an event and inviting people to attend, you can reach a large number of potential clients for free. Why not organise a group dog walk for a charity and then you'll have lots of information about local dog owners who could be potential clients!

Facebook Marketplace is also a great way to reach potential clients. This is a platform where people can buy and sell items, and it's perfect for promoting dog walking services. Simply create a listing for your business, and be sure to include all the relevant information potential clients will need, such as your price, contact details, and location.

In addition, you can use Facebook's paid advertising options to reach a wider audience. While there is a cost associated with this option, you can set a budget that works for you. And with the ability to target your ads by location, interests, and other factors, you can be sure that your ads are reaching the people most likely to use your services.

Get involved with your local dog walking community

There are numerous ways to get involved with your local dog walking community. One great way is to become a volunteer for a local dog shelter or rescue organisation.

Most of these organisations are always in need of volunteers to help care for the dogs in their shelters. By volunteering, you will not only be able to walk the dogs, but you will also be able to help with other activities such as feeding, grooming, and exercising them.

In addition, you will also have the opportunity to meet other dog lovers in your community and build relationships with them.

Another way to get involved with your local dog walking community is to join a local dog walking group. These groups typically meet on a regular basis to walk dogs together and are open to the public. This is a great way to meet other dog walkers in your area and build relationships with them.

In addition, it provides you with the opportunity to promote your business to others in the group. You can do this subtly by just wearing your branded sweatshirt, and make sure you have plenty of business cards to hand in your dog walking bag!

Make yourself available for interviews with local newspapers and radio

If you're looking for a way to advertise your dog-related business for free, consider making yourself available for interviews with local newspapers and radio stations. Talk about your dogs and what makes them special. Share stories about your experiences with dogs. Offer tips on how to care for dogs.

By doing this, you'll be promoting your business while also helping to educate the public about dogs. In addition, you may also find that you develop a following of loyal clients who appreciate your knowledge and expertise.

Write an article for your local newspaper about the benefits of using a dog walker for busy owners

Writing an article for your local newspaper is a great way to advertise your business for free. Not only will you reach a wide audience, but you'll also be able to show off your expertise on a given topic.

If you're not sure where to start, consider writing about your new business and what it offers, or an upcoming event that your business is hosting. You can also use the article to highlight why you're different and what you're offering.

Whatever you choose to write about, be sure to keep it newsworthy and interesting. Remember, the goal is to capture the attention of potential clients and encourage them to patronise your business. With a little effort, you can use this simple marketing technique to boost your bottom line.

For example, how about writing something on a topic like this...

"*Being a busy pet owner doesn't have to mean your furry friend misses out on regular walks. In fact, hiring a dog walker can be beneficial for both you and your pet. For instance, dog walking provides much-needed exercise and stimulation, which can help to reduce behavioural problems such as barking and chewing.*

What's more, dog walking can also be a great way to socialise your pet, helping them to interact confidently with other dogs and people. And of course, it's always nice to come home to a tired puppy who is happy to snuggle up on the couch rather than bouncing off the walls! If you're thinking of using a dog walker, why not get in touch."

Making a pitch to the media can be daunting, but if you look online you'll find the editors email address and you can send your article over with your contact details. For detailed advice on how to do this, see the resources section at the end of this book!

Attend pet-related events in your area

Pet-related events can be great opportunities to advertise your business for free. You can go in person wearing your branded sweatshirts and a pocket full of business cards, or take a small stand. Fees are usually very low for local events and even village fetes can be a good place to start and get your face and name known.

In addition, take advantage of any speaking opportunities that may arise. For example, you could give a brief talk about the services you offer or offer a demonstration of your work. By taking advantage of these free advertising opportunities, you can help to ensure that more people are aware of your business and what you have to offer.

Free Ad sites

If you're looking for a way to promote your dog walking business, why not try using free ad websites? By creating a simple ad, you can reach a wide audience of potential clients. Be sure to include your contact information and rates, and be sure to mention any special services that you offer.

You may also want to include a photo of yourself with one of your dogs. Remember, the goal is to make your ad stand out from the rest. With a little effort, you'll be surprised at how many new clients you can attract. Sites like Gumtree and Craigslist are ideal. For more sites, check out the Resources at the end of this book.

Use your email signature

There's a simple way to promote your business that you may not have thought of: your email signature. Every time you send an email, your recipients will see your signature, and it only takes a few seconds to add a link to your website or social media page. You can even include a brief tagline or some client testimonials to give recipients a taste of what you do. Best of all, this promotion is completely free.

So, if you're looking for a quick and easy way to get the word out about your dog walking business, start by adding a signature to your emails. If you want to be really swish, check out the tools I recommend to make your signature really engaging and working hard for you! (see the Resources at the end of this book).

Word of Mouth

As a professional dog walker, one of the most important things you can do to promote your business is to build positive relationships with your clients. One way to do this is by providing excellent service and maintaining clear communication. If your clients are happy with your service, they are more likely to tell their friends and family about you.

Referrals or word of mouth marketing is the best marketing because people who have used your services and know just how wonderful you are will tell others. Added bonus – it's free. Ask your clients for a testimonial and use these in your online and other marketing.

Give out flyers and business cards to local businesses

There are many ways to advertise your business, but some methods can be quite costly. If you're on a tight budget, you'll be happy to know that there are places online where you can print business cards and flyers at very low cost. Once you've got them, you can get the word out about your business by giving out your flyers and business cards to local businesses.

Make sure to target businesses that are frequented by your target market. For example, you might want to leave flyers and business cards at the dog groomers, pet stores, veterinary clinics, and dog parks.

If you have large employers near you, contact their HR department and see if you can put a flyer in the canteen or staff room. Even better, if you have a friend who works there, ask them to do it for you!

You can also ask other highstreet businesses if they would be willing to display your marketing materials. Some may charge a small fee, but many will be willing to help support you, especially if you take some of their leaflets and give them to your clients in exchange.

By taking advantage of free advertising opportunities like this, you can reach your target market without breaking the bank.

Resources

I understand that starting a dog walking business can be a daunting task. That's why I've created a helpful resources section to give you the information and tools you need to get started. Click on the link below to access my growing list of tools, freebies, references, organisations and more.

https://www.rufflesnuffle.co.uk/resources-for-dog-walkers/

Don't miss out!

Visit the website below and you can sign up to receive emails whenever Sarah-Jane White publishes a new book. There's no charge and no Obligation.

https://books2read.com/r/B-A-JWAS-LZKWB

Connecting independent readers to independent writers.

About the Author

Sarah-Jane White is an Animal Behaviourist. She lives in Norfolk with her family on a small farm.Her mission is to help pet parents use enrichment for a happy and fulfilling life together. Sarah-Jane regularly shares ideas that support the instinctual behaviours of their pets in safe, fun, and enriching ways every day. She runs award-winning business Ruffle Snuffle®

Read more at https://www.rufflesnuffle.co.uk.

Printed in Great Britain
by Amazon

16121468R00061